# *Golfing* WITH GOD

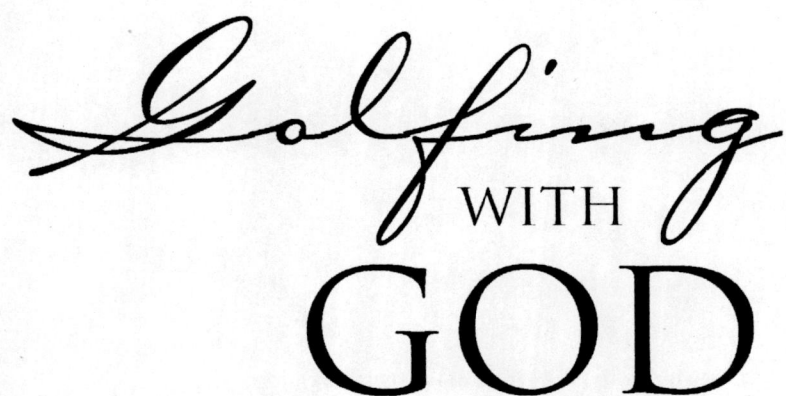

# WITH
# GOD

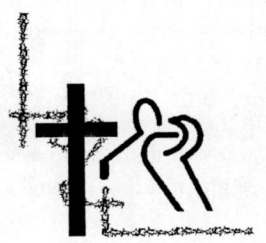

DOUGLAS W. TATRO

© 2003 by Douglas Tatro. All rights reserved.

Printed in the United States of America

Packaged by Pleasant Word, a division of WinePress Publishing, PO Box 428, Enumclaw, WA 98022. The views expressed or implied in this work do not necessarily reflect those of Pleasant Word, a division of WinePress Publishing. Ultimate design, content, and editorial accuracy of this work are the responsibilities of the author.

No part of this publication may be reproduced, stored in a retrieval system, or transmitted in any way by any means—electronic, mechanical, photocopy, recording, or otherwise—without the prior permission of the copyright holder, except as provided by USA copyright law.

Unless otherwise noted, all Scriptures are taken from the Holy Bible, New International Version, Copyright © 1973, 1978, 1984 by the International Bible Society. Used by permission of Zondervan Publishing House. The "NIV" and "New International Version" trademarks are registered in the United States Patent and Trademark Office by International Bible Society.

Scripture references marked NKJV are taken from the New King James Version, Copyright © 1979, 1980, 1982 by Thomas Nelson, Inc., Publishers. Used by permission.

ISBN 1-57921-642-0
Library of Congress Catalog Card Number: 2003103417

Photographs are courtesy of Ken Andrews Photography.

Special thanks are extended to:
Diamond Hill Golf and Country Club Dover, Florida for allowing us to use photographs of their great facility.

We would like to thank ParView, Inc. for sharing the photographs of their Global Positioning System.

The Golfing With God Logo was designed by Patricia Tatro.

# Dedication

I would like to dedicate this book to the memory of my grandmother, Ruth W. Bailey. To me, along with my brothers and sister, she was Ninny. (That rhymes with skinny.) When Ninny was in high school she graduated as valedictorian of her class. Although she never went on to further her education, because it wasn't fashionable back in those days, she was by far one of the most intelligent people I have had the pleasure to know. My mother, aunt, and two uncles may not have always appreciated their mother's intelligence as they were growing up, but she was my grandmother, and we all know how grandchildren think about their grandparents.

When I was in junior high school I developed a desire to write, although back then it was mostly poetry. Ninny encouraged me to always carry a pad of paper and a pencil with me so that whenever an idea came into my head, I could capture it on paper immediately. I didn't always remember to carry the paper and pencil but I never forgot the encouragement she gave me. I'll never forget too, how she would come to my defense with my mom when I was being a typical mischievous young boy—something I did a great deal.

When Ninny died I wrote a poem to her that was read at her funeral. I would like to conclude by repeating just a few of the lines from that poem.

> Ninny, for all the things you've ever done, and the unknown things you'll do, this one's written special, this one's just for you.

Douglas W. Tatro

# Table of Contents

Preface ............................................................. 13

Chapter 1: Let's Tee Off ................................... 19
Chapter 2: Now Let's Tee Off ............................ 25
    The Starter ................................................. 25
    The Tee Box ............................................... 28
    Choosing the Right Club ............................ 31
    Tee It Up ..................................................... 37
Chapter 3: Playing the Game ............................ 41
    Fairway Verses Rough ................................. 41
    Avoid the Hazards ...................................... 46
    Unavoidable Hazards ................................. 52
Chapter 4: On the Green .................................. 59
    Survey the Putt ........................................... 59
    Lag It Up There ........................................... 65
    It's a Gimmie—Or Is It? .............................. 69
Chapter 5: Odds and Ends ................................ 79
    Too Big for My Britches (And Not from Eating) ...... 79
    Thank God for Mulligans ............................ 84
    The Refreshment Cart ................................ 89
    Have You Used Your GPS Today? ............... 93
    Some Final Thoughts ................................. 98

All scripture is quoted from the King James Version, unless otherwise noted. Contemporary words have been substituted in some circumstances for clarity. Other translations used are:

NKJV - New King James Version
NIV - New International Version

# Preface

Six o'clock in the morning. My brother Bob and I are already up, dressed, and in the process of having breakfast. We're preparing to go to work. Two brothers going to work doesn't sound very unusual and it wasn't, except for the fact that we were fourteen and ten years old respectively. We were on our way to the golf course to caddie. Bob started a couple of years before me but now we both carried the bags of Greater Boston's finest golfers. We thought they were good golfers. In retrospect they were probably average duffers just like many of us today.

Caddying was my first introduction to the world of golf. I really enjoyed caddying, not because of any great love for golf; that came later. I was only ten years old but I was becoming rich or at least I thought I was. I would get paid $3.00 for carrying a person's bag around for eighteen holes. If I was lucky, I could caddy once in the morning and once in the afternoon. WOW! I was making $6.00 a day and I was just a kid. The older boys, like my brother, did even better than I did. They could carry doubles (two bags, one on each shoulder) and make $6.00 per round or $12.00 on a good day.

I know you're probably wondering why the members at this rather exclusive golf course would pay these runny-nosed kids to carry their bags? Why didn't they just rent a golf cart and not have to put up with us dragging behind, peeing in the bushes, and not seeing in what direction their ball went? Golf carts were just becoming popular and they were expensive to rent. Only the wealthiest of the wealthy rented a cart. It was cheaper to pay the teenage mules than to rent a cart. I was glad the members wanted caddies. It made me feel like I was as wealthy as they were. In addition, it helped pay for summer camp on a couple of occasions and contributed toward my first year of college.

One afternoon a week the members allowed the caddies to play golf. I used some of the riches I had accumulated from caddying to buy my first set of golf clubs. I purchased a beginner's set of Jack Thompson Signature clubs. These were my weapons to attack the same golf-ball-swallowing hazards as the members I caddied for. They included a driver, three wood, three, five, seven, and nine irons, plus a putter. I proudly swung those clubs for many years before adding mongrel clubs to fill in the set and eventually, buying a second hand set of matched clubs. This was my introduction to the game that I've never been really good at, but for some reason love with a passion.

During those same years when I began my love affair with golf, I was developing another passion far greater and more important than any other in my life. My love for Christ

## Preface

didn't start with a passion, that's for sure. I grew up in a home where going to church wasn't an option. It was just automatic. I could better describe our option to go to church as, you do or you die. I didn't mind going to church. After all, I had several friends there to hang out with. My early memories of church are exactly that—a place my mom took us on Sunday mornings where I could play with the friends I didn't see at school. Play is the key word in that last sentence.

My family wouldn't let me get by without telling about my third grade Sunday school class. What a group we had, a few innocent girls and several high-spirited boys! We weren't bad kids, just high-spirited like I said. We were so high-spirited however, that before the year was half over the teacher quit in desperation. I wish now I could apologize for our behavior back then. If only the teacher knew all the seeds that he really had sown. My own dad believed in God, and in his younger days helped established a Bible class in his hometown. I really think he knew Christ as his Savior, but for as long as I could remember; he only went to church on Christmas, Easter, and special occasions when one of us in his family was doing something. Mom was the one who made sure we had religion, whether we liked it or not.

Mom may have made sure we had religion in our lives, but that didn't insure any type of understanding or commitment on our part. Seeds were planted however, and the Holy Spirit had our attention, even if it was only for short spans at any given time. When children in our church reached approximately twelve years of age, they would take confirmation classes. Confirmation classes were where you learned church history, doctrine, and prepared to become a member of the church. When I started confirmation classes, Mom must have grown weary of fighting with me about it because she finally let me drop out. I just wasn't interested and consequently didn't pay attention or learn my lessons. I have to believe that God must have given my Mom special wisdom in dealing with me, not just in this circumstance, but also in many throughout my life. I, unfortunately, wasn't ready to make a commitment to Jesus.

Only a few years later confirmation meant so much more to me. I don't know whether it was natural maturation or the Holy Spirit quietly working within me but when I reached high school, I came to the realization that I needed a clear understanding of God in my life. I was confirmed with a group of adults and developed a faith within me that still serves as the basis for the person I am today. I even considered going into the ministry when I graduated from high school. Notice I still haven't mentioned any type of commitment to the Lord Jesus. My faith was growing, but I had a long way to go before I really understood what the Bible was so clearly trying to tell me.

While I was at Boston University studying to be a physical education teacher, our minister asked if I would organize and coach a church basketball team. I was happy to do anything that was in my field of study, so I accepted the challenge gladly. After coaching the church basketball team for two years, I was asked if I'd be interested in supervising the junior and senior high youth groups. My faith in God was still growing and this was a paid position that would certainly help me as a college student, so I enthusiastically accepted. Even though the Sunday school classes were not part of my responsibility, I tried to support all areas of ministry within the church. My desire to be supportive led me to attend a Good Friday service presented by the kindergarten classes. In that simple little program, put on by four and five-year-old children, I realized how much God loved me, and I realized the sacrifice that Jesus made on my behalf. I left that service and went to my office where I cried as hard as I ever had. I prayed to God, asking Him to forgive me of my sins, and asking Jesus to be my Lord and Savior. I finally understood what the Bible was trying to say to me all along and I now could insert my name into John 3:16 and say:

> *For God so loved Doug Tatro that he gave his only begotten Son, and if Doug Tatro believes in Him, he shall not perish but have everlasting life.*

My walk with Christ has not always been smooth. I have fallen away and come crawling back asking God's forgiveness more than once. Today, I am far from perfect but I know in whom I believeth and in whom I pledge my faith because of grace I don't deserve. Because my walk with the Lord is closer today than ever before, I can look around and see God at work in my life wherever I go and in whatever I do, even when I'm playing golf. This book has given me the opportunity to examine my life more closely and to share with you many of my observations, not on my life but on how I see God in all that I do. Writing this book has helped me step up onto another rung on the ladder, to help me draw closer to my Lord and Savior. I pray that you, the reader, can realize a portion of the closeness that I feel within these words.

Now let's tee off. I just love a good game of golf, especially when I'm golfing with God.

## Chapter 1

# Let's Tee Off

Romans 13:12
*The night is far spent, the day is at hand; let us therefore cast off the works of darkness, and let us put on the armour of light.*

I would like to share two different scenarios for beginning a round of golf. Even if you have never played golf before, you should be able to identify the difference between the two and make an educated guess as to the preferred circumstances for beginning a day on the links.

Yahoo! I pull into the parking lot of the golf course. I've anticipated this for two days now. I've cleaned my clubs, my shoes, and bought a new sleeve of balls. I drop my bag off at the bag drop (that seems like the logical place to drop off my bag), and walk into the pro shop to verify my tee time and pay my greens fees. So far so good. I drive my golf cart around to pick up my bag of clubs, which I left at the bag drop, unless I'm at a more exclusive golf course where they have someone put your bag on the cart for you. I put on my shoes, take a couple of my new golf balls, put a few tees in my pocket, and away I go to the first tee to begin my conquest for this day. This is scenario Number One. Now let's take a look at scenario number two.

Yahoo! I pull into the parking lot of the golf course. I've anticipated this for two days now. I've cleaned my clubs, my shoes, and bought a new sleeve of balls. I drop my bag off at the bag drop (that seems like the logical place to drop off my bag), and walk into the pro shop to verify my tee time and pay my greens fees. So far so good. I drive my golf cart around to pick up my bag of clubs, which I left at the bag drop, unless I'm at a more exclusive golf course where they have someone put your bag on the cart for you. I put on my shoes, put a few tees in my pocket, and away I go to the practice tee to warm up for my conquest of this day.

I've laid out the two scenarios for you. Which makes more sense to you? Hopefully, it doesn't take a brain surgeon to understand that I should go to the practice tee to warm up. Baseball players warm up before a game. Football players, tennis players, bowlers, bocce players, and virtually all athletes in nearly all sports warm up before they begin to play.

So off I go to the practice tee to warm up before I begin my round of golf. Out comes the pitching wedge first. For all you non-golfers, the pitching wedge only hits the ball short distances. I swing easily, hit that range ball straight as an arrow about seventy-five to a hundred yards and my warm-up has begun. (Notice that since I'm writing this, my ball went straight as an arrow. In real life the ball may or may not go straight as an arrow, but I believe I'm allowed writer's privileges in fantasizing as much as I want.)

After hitting a few more wedge shots, I take out the seven iron, then the five, and the three. Next I pull out my three wood to hit a few balls. Finally I finish with the big kahuna: the driver—the club that hits the ball the farthest of all the clubs in my bag. My warm-up doesn't end with hitting the driver though. Now I walk to the putting green. I take out my putter and practice for ten to fifteen more minutes. I hit long putts, short putts, and in-between putts. I hit putts that are uphill, downhill, putts that curve right and curve left. Now, and only now, I think I'm ready to assault the enemy on this given day.

Athletes from all nations around the world, of all ages, male and female, in practically all sports, know you should warm up before you begin to actually participate. Why then, does the average person head out the door every morning without doing the same thing? I don't mean warm up to participate in a sport. I mean warm up to begin the day. Athletes will spend numerous minutes or hours warming up, but most people don't have the same amount of common sense to warm up for their day.

Just as I referred to my golf game as the enemy of the day or my conquest for the day, each of us better understand that spiritual warfare goes on each and every day of our lives. Satan is constantly trying to interrupt our days and place a wedge between the Lord and us. If you don't believe it, take a look at your day, a good, hard, honest look. What about that attractive secretary or boss you stared at with more than a casual glance? What about that circumstance that caused you to lose your temper and maybe even use the Lord's name in vain? What about the car you cut off in traffic because you were in a hurry and felt it was your turn to go no matter what? (That was a yellow light, I believe). These are only a few general examples of ways that Satan disrupts your day and separates you from your heavenly Father. Your circumstances may be totally different from these I've used, but I know that if you really look at your day, you too can see where Satan is trying his utmost to get a foothold in your life.

Hopefully, I've convinced you that we all need to warm up before we start our day. And hopefully, your next question is going to be, "How does one warm up to begin the day?"

I'm glad you asked that question; I thought you might. Everyone should have some part of his or her day put aside for private time with God. Private time is an opportunity for you to pray, study God's word, and grow closer to Him. The morning is an excellent opportunity to have your private time because it starts your day off on the right foot, it warms you up for the day, and it prepares you mentally and spiritually for all the challenges you will encounter throughout your day.

Unfortunately I know the morning isn't the most convenient time for some people to have their private time. We shouldn't blame people if they can't have their private time in the morning. Some people have children they need to get off to school, or spouses they need to get off to work. Some people don't function well in the morning. (We all know people like that.) If you're not a morning person then you certainly shouldn't have your private time in the morning, because we want to give God our best. If that's later in the day then make it later in the day. If for any number of reasons you can't have your private time in the morning, then at the very least have a short prayer time. Everyone can find the time to pray in the morning, even if you have children or a spouse to get out the door by a certain time.

Morning prayer is a great family activity. Just imagine what the world would be like if all husbands and wives took the time to pray together each morning. Imagine how our homes and our communities would be if every family took the time to pray together each morning.

Ephesians 6:11&17 says:

*Put on the whole armour of God, that ye may be able to stand against the wiles of the devil. And take the helmet of salvation, and the sword of the Spirit, which is the word of God.*

Not only will morning prayer time or private time help us put on the armor of God and prepare us for our daily battles with Satan, it also draws us closer to God.

John 14:21 (NKJV) says:

*He that has my commandments, and keeps them, he it is that loves me: and he that loves me shall be loved of my Father, and I will love him, and will manifest myself to him.*

My pastor tells our church family, "If you are filled with the Holy Spirit, there isn't any place for Satan to take a foot hold." I can't think of a better way to be sure that I'm filled with the Holy Spirit than to begin each day either with private time or with prayer time. If athletes recognize the need to warm up before they begin their activity then certainly we, God's people, should recognize the need to warm up before we begin our day. There is a popular saying going around that says, "If God said it, I believe it, that's all there is to it." Well, God's word tells us the importance of studying the word and praying. Let's all start our day in communion with God. It's a great way to warm up.

**Put on the whole armor of God, that ye may be able to stand against the wiles of the devil**

**Ephesians 6:11**

# Chapter 2

# Now Let's Tee Off

### THE STARTER

Psalm 71: 17
*O, God thou has taught me from youth: and hitherto have I declared thy wondrous works. Now also when I am old and grey headed, O GOD, forsake me not; until I have shewed thy strength unto this generation, and thy power to every one that is to come.*

I'm all warmed up and ready to begin today's round of golf. I drive my golf cart over to the first tee and report to the starter. The starter is the person who checks to make sure it's your turn to begin. He controls the flow of play by the amount of time between each group of golfers. The starters are usually friendly and if it's your first time on the course, will tell you about any ground rules or hazards you should know. The starter can really make your day on the course far better, depending on the advice he or she gives you.

The starter can easily be thought of as a mentor. That is someone, usually older but not always, who can give advice and share his or her wisdom with you. The Bible recognizes the need for mentors and exhorts people to not only listen to, but also respect our elders.
1 Peter 5:5 says:

> *Likewise, ye younger, submit yourselves unto the elder. Yea, all of you be subject one to another.*

Hopefully your church has a mentoring ministry, but if it doesn't you can still seek out an older person or friend to whom you can be accountable. The elders of the church should cherish the role of mentor. They have experiences younger church members have not yet encountered. Elders have wisdom that only time can develop. Many ministries for women have received the idea of mentoring favorably and have actually been doing it in some form for many years. The men of the church have not tutored each other as well as they should have. That's not to say there aren't some churches that have implemented mentoring programs for men, but unfortunately, they are the exception, not the rule. With all the worldly temptations facing each and every one of us on a daily basis, imagine what a blessing it would be to be able to call on someone you trust and respect, and with whom you could discuss these situations. Younger men should cherish the opportunity to serve as spiritual apprentices under older more experienced Christian men. Those same older men should seize that same opportunity to contribute to the spiritual growth of the church.

# Now Let's Tee Off

1 Timothy 5:17 says:

*Let the elders that rule well be counted worthy of double honour, especially they who labour in the word and doctrine.*

Just as the starter on the golf course can help you avoid hazards along the way, a mentor can help you avoid the hazards of life. If your church doesn't have a mentoring program, look into starting one. If starting a mentoring program isn't viable for your church at this time, at least find your own personal mentor to help you grow in your spiritual life.

**Likewise ye younger, submit yourselves unto the elder. Yea, all of you be subject one to another, . . .**

1 Peter 5:5

## The Tee Box

Romans 12: 10
*Be kindly affectioned one to another with brotherly love; in honour preferring one another.*

The Starter has finally said it is my turn to launch today's assault on the course. I pull my golf cart up to the tee box on the first tee. Tee box is the name given to the area where golfers hit their first shot on each hole. The tee or tee box is a flat plot, usually slightly elevated. On the tee box is a series of colored markers. The markers indicate where the golfers are to hit from, depending upon their ability. Sometimes there will be one large tee box with the markers lined up several yards apart and sometimes there will actually be smaller separate tee boxes with the different colored markers identifying each level of golfing competency. The colored markers on the tee box are coordinated with the same colors on the scorecards so the golfers can read how many yards it is from the tee to the green. The green, for all you non-golfers, is where the hole is located. Typical colors used on the tee box markers are red, white, blue, and gold. Some golf courses use other colors and some of the more exclusive courses, I mentioned before, use very ornate tee markers.

When I look at those markers, identifying the various levels of a golfer's ability, I see a Christian walk with the Lord, a walk that each of us has taken and continues to take each day. The red markers compare to the new Christian, the newborn in the Lord, those who have just begun their walk.

## Now Let's Tee Off

The Bible says in 1 Peter 2:2&3:

*As newborn babes, desire the sincere milk of the word, that ye may grow thereby: If so be ye have tasted that the Lord is gracious.*

Just as the markers on the tee box identify the time and effort that golfers have sacrificed to raise their level of play, Christians need to continually apply the same intensity in order to raise their level of faith to move closer and closer to the Lord. Every Christian should strive to move further up the ladder and at the same time be helping those newer in their walk with the Lord God—just like the maintenance men on the golf course provide markers for you to identify the level of your game. Unlike the markers on the golf course however, we never reach the highest level. None of us, not one, is exempt from sin and is without room for growth. Continue your walk with the Lord, striving always to raise your level of play. Rejoice, encourage, and tutor the new Christians as they raise their level also.

2 Thessalonians 1:3 (NIV) says:

*We ought always to thank God for you, brothers, and rightly so, because your faith is growing more and more, and the love every one of you has for each other is increasing.*

Now Let's Tee Off

## Choosing the Right Club

1 Peter 1: 24 & 25
*For all flesh is as grass, and all the glory of man as the flowers of grass. The grass withereth, and the flower thereof falleth away: But the word of the Lord endureth forever. And this is the word which by the gospel is preached to you.*

Finally I'm on the tee. I look down the fairway and ask myself, "Mmm, what club should I use to put myself in good position?" For all you non-golfers, let me take a moment to explain the difference between the various clubs.

The irons in a golf bag are numbered from one to nine. Not many golfers carry a one iron, but they are made and a few people do use them. The difference in the clubs is the amount of loft (pitch) in the head (the hitting part). The lower numbered clubs have the least amount of loft and therefore hit the ball lower and farther. As the clubs go up in number, the loft increases; therefore the ball goes higher and shorter.

Along with irons one through nine, most golfers also carry a pitching wedge and a sand wedge. Some golfers may also carry an additional wedge for special circumstances. A pitching wedge is used for hitting the ball short distances and hitting the ball very high if needed. A sand wedge is designed to specifically hit the ball out of the sand, but can be used at other times to hit the ball short distances.

In some golfers' bag, you'll also find three or four woods. I still call them woods because that's what they used to be made of. Today they are made of metal but old habits are hard to break. Most golfers carry a driver, the club I earlier referred to as the Big Kahuna. The driver is used primarily off the tee and is designed to hit the ball long distances. The driver is also the hardest club to hit well. For this reason beginning golfers should consider hitting something else from the tee, but few understand that and still want to use their driver. Along with the driver, most golfers carry two or three fairway woods. The fairway woods, as the name implies, are used primarily in the fairway. The difference in the fairway woods, just as with the irons, is the amount of loft on the face of the club. The final club in any golfer's bag is the putter. The putter is used to putt, or hit, the ball when on the green and trying to get the ball into the hole. As you can see, there is basically a different club for each situation on the golf course. Now, back to my original question, "Mmm, What club should I use?"

Come to think of it, my set of clubs makes me think of what my Bible is for me in my daily life. No matter what, there is a scripture for that situation.

2 Timothy 3:16&17 says:

> *All scripture is given by inspiration of God, and is profitable for doctrine, for reproof, for correction, for instruction in righteousness: That the man of God may be perfect, thoroughly furnished unto all good works.*

The way I read the previous scripture, it sounds like the Bible has all I need to face any problem, any situation, any day. Wow, what great news! God has given me a manual that explains exactly how to handle all my problems and cares, in fact, how to handle my whole life. That is great news, but unfortunately there are still people who don't understand it or choose to ignore it. It's amazing to me that

## Now Let's Tee Off

when people buy a new piece of machinery, whether it's a lawn mower, a dishwasher, a blender, or any other sort of appliance, they usually read the manual to make sure they use and maintain it properly. However, the Bible, the manual on life that's been given by God himself to help us use and maintain our lives, is unfortunately one of the biggest dust collectors in many homes. We've been placed here on earth

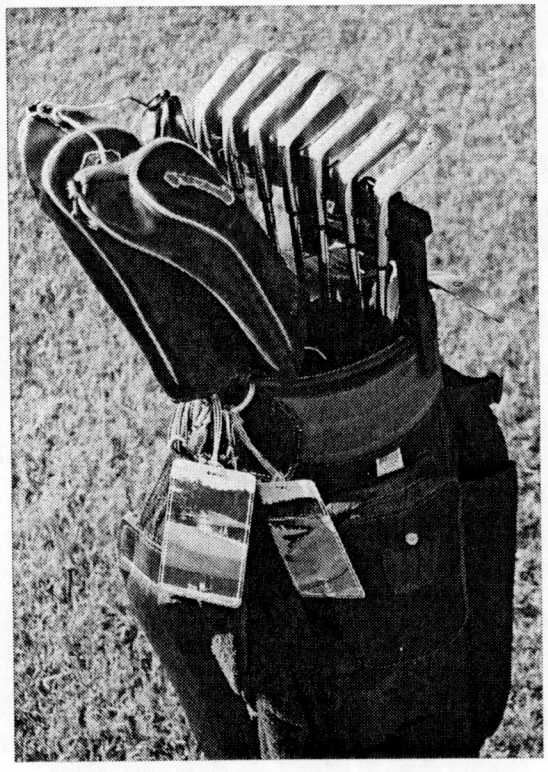

**All scripture is given by inspiration of God, and is profitable for doctrine, for reproof, for correction, for instruction in rightousness: that the man of God may be perfect, throughly furnished unto all good works.**
**2 Timothy 3:16, 17**

for one reason: to serve God. If we do that, according to the instruction book that he has provided, he rewards us. He rewards us with blessings we don't deserve, but by His grace, He provides anyway because of the love He has for us. Does that sound too good to be true? Follow the instruction manual and be blessed. That's the way it is, believe it or not.

Here are some simple tips to help you start reading the Bible on a regular basis so you can understand the simple plan God has for your life. First, make the time available to read the Bible. We all make time for the things that are important in our lives. Certainly serving God and obeying His will for our lives should rank right up there with things that are important. All of us, if we're honest with ourselves, can and should find some time each day to spend with the Lord. Most people can find a half hour, ten or fifteen minutes, or even five minutes here and there. We all can find the time if it is a priority.

Second, find a Bible you can understand. I had trouble understanding all the *thee's* and *thou's* when I first read the Bible. However, there are several translations of the Bible available today that are written in vocabulary all of us can understand. My wife has a great way of looking at this and it fits right in with my analogy of the training manual. The manuals that come with new appliances usually are printed in different languages. You have to find the one you understand.

Some people are probably cringing as I tell you to find a readable translation of the Bible because they believe in reading only the King James Version. Now that I understand the Bible better, I appreciate the King James, but it's a tough

## Now Let's Tee Off

place to start and it too is a translation. If we didn't believe in reading different translations of the Bible we would all have to know how to read Latin, Greek, and Hebrew so we could read the original manuscripts. My only caution is to consult someone such as your pastor, minister, priest, or other clergyman who can advise you as to what translations are the most accurate in expressing the true meaning of God's Word.

Third, carry the Bible with you at all times. This means, not necessarily your personal Bible you bring to church and use during your private time, but some form of the scriptures. You might want to carry a pocket version of the New Testament, or, what I really like is a pocket Book of Promises. A Book of Promises is a book in which someone else has categorized various scriptures from the Bible according to real life situations. When you open the book, simply find the section you need at that particular moment. There are sections such as: when you're happy, when you're sad, when you're angry, confused, feeling guilty, overjoyed, and so on. Promise books are a great supplement to your scripture reading. However, don't make the mistake of only reading your promise book in lieu of the Bible itself. Be sure to read the complete Bible to enjoy the full text of the scriptures.

John 5:39 says:

*Search the scriptures; for in them ye think ye have eternal life: and they are they which testify of me.*

One final thought about the Bible in my life and hopefully yours: nothing can enhance your understanding of the Bible like attendance at a local scripture-based church. Interaction in a Bible Fellowship class, Bible Study, or Sunday School, along with hearing the word in God-inspired messages from the preacher make church membership essential to a healthy walk with the Lord. Search the scriptures and allow the Holy Spirit to assist in whatever situation you find yourself.

Let's see now . . . what club was I going to use for this particular shot?

Now Let's Tee Off

## Tee It Up

Matthew 7: 7&8
*Ask, and it shall be given you; seek and you shall find; knock, and it shall be opened unto you: For every one that asketh receiveth; and he that seeketh findeth; and to him that knocketh it shall be opened.*

The starter has given us the OK to begin. We've driven up to the tee box. I've selected the correct club for this particular hole. Now it's time to "tee up the ball" and see what happens with my first shot of the day. "Tee up the ball"—that's an expression many of us have heard quite often. We don't think much about it because we understand what the expression means.

Imagine for a moment that you were totally ignorant about golf and everything to do with golf. "Tee up the ball, I wonder what that could mean? I know, I'll take a marker and put little letter T's all over the ball, then it will be all T'd up." Having a ball with little letter T's all over it would be good for me. After all, my last name begins with the letter T. When I go searching the woods for my ball, as I very often do, it will be easy to identify with all the T's on it.

No, no, no; that's not what "tee it up" means. Maybe teeing up the ball is something I have to do the night before my golf game. First I brew a nice pot of warm tea. Second, I soak the golf balls in the tea over night so they'll be all tea'd up. Having golf balls soaked in tea must help them roll better or something. These two theories of what it must mean to tee up the ball are absolutely ridiculous and really serve no purpose other than to help us focus on what the real meaning is in the expression "tee up the ball."

Once again, for all you non-golfers, to "tee up the ball" means the ball is placed on a small pedestal, usually made of wood or plastic. Golfers are allowed to use a tee only when hitting from the tee box at the beginning of each hole. Before the use of plastic and prior to mass production of wooden tees, golfers would gather a small mound of dirt and place the ball on it using it as a tee. I wasn't around in the days of dirt tees but it's not hard to believe. Even today as I play golf, I see people on all parts of the course moving their ball onto a little mound of dirt or grass to tee it up. Many of you are laughing because you know exactly what

> Thou shalt make thy prayers unto him, and He shall hear thee . . .
> Job 22:27

## Now Let's Tee Off

I'm talking about. I know, what does it hurt to tee the ball up on a tuft of grass? After all it's just a friendly game with a group of buddies. There's nothing wrong with it as long as what's fair for one is fair for all. I wouldn't try playing preferred lies, that is, placing the ball in a better location, in a tournament either. It will cost you several penalty strokes.

So why do players like using a tee off the tee box and anywhere else they can get away with it? Golfers can hit the ball "cleaner" when it is up on a tee. The cleaner, or better, a golfer hits the ball, the more chance that golfer has to hit a good shot. It's simple—tee the ball up for cleaner, better shots that produce better results when playing.

By now I'm sure you are wondering, where's the analogy? What does a tee or the expression "tee the ball up" have to do with God or the Bible? The ball is raised on a tee to improve the chances of hitting a good shot. When we lift our daily concerns up in prayer, we improve our relationship with God. When we lift our daily concerns up in prayer, we prepare the way for the Holy Spirit to go before us. When we lift our daily concerns up in prayer, we improve our shot at living in God's will.

Job 22:27 says:

*Thou shalt make thy prayer unto Him, and He shall hear thee.*

Deuteronomy 1:30 says:

*The Lord your God which goeth before you, He shall fight for you, according to all that He did for you in Egypt before your eyes.*

What reassurance those two scriptures hold. When you lift up your prayers to God, He will hear you. Second, God will go before you and fight for you. Think for a moment how profound those statements are. When I lift up my concerns, my praise, and my problems, God, the creator of all things, takes the time to hear my voice. This expression may date me, but that just blows my mind. Better yet, God will go before me and fight my battles. That's like betting on a horse race after it's over. When we put our concerns in God's hands, we know his will shall be done.

Lifting up the ball with a tee improves your chances of a good shot. Lifting up your prayers to the Lord assures you of your best shot.

I'm ready to send that ball down the fairway. All right, take the club back slowly; keep my eye on the ball, lead with my left arm, and POW. There goes the ball, right down the middle of the fairway. Remember, I'm allowed to fantasize each and every shot. At least in this book I am.

# Chapter 3
# Playing the Game

### FAIRWAY VERSES ROUGH

2 Corinthians 6: 4–10
*But in all things approving ourselves as the ministers of God, in much patience, in afflictions, in necessities, in distresses, in stripes, in imprisonments, in tumults, in labours, in watchings, in fastings; by pureness, by knowledge, by longsuffering, by kindness, by the Holy Ghost, by love unfeigned, by the word of truth, by the power of God, by the armour of righteousness on the right hand and on the left, by honour and dishonour, by evil report and good report: as deceivers, and yet true; as unknown, and yet well known; as dying, and, behold, we live; as chastened, and not killed; as sorrowful, yet alway rejoicing; as poor, yet making many rich; as having nothing, and yet possessing all things.*

Right down the middle of the fairway. Not bad for my first shot of the day. Anyone who knows anything about golf will tell you, the more fairways you hit and stay in, the better you will score. Staying in the fairway is so important that even professional golfers keep track of fairways they hit. Why is it so important to keep your ball in the fairway? If you've ever walked around a golf course, even if it was just to attend a wedding reception in the clubhouse, you know what the attraction is in the fairways. The fairways are beautiful, well-manicured grass. The fairways are generally smooth and easy places from which to hit a golf ball. Hitting your first shot in the fairway makes your second shot much easier.

What's the alternative to hitting the ball in the fairway? Hitting the ball in the rough. Just the name rough should be an indication of what your life will be like if you hit the ball there. The grass in the rough is much longer than the grass in the fairway. Sometimes the grass is so long in the rough that it's difficult to find the ball. I have no doubt that if golf balls had human qualities, several of them that I have hit were probably laughing at me as I walked right past them. When you do find the ball, then you have the task of trying to hit it out of the rough. The long grass prevents the club from making good contact with the ball, and in general, you just have a rough shot.

Occasionally aiming over or toward the rough is very tempting. On a hole that doglegs, or turns either right or left, sometimes you can take several yards off the length of the hole by hitting over the rough. If you're successful in cutting the corner, the next shot should be easier. Obviously, cutting corners sounds tempting at times. Unfortunately, if your shot over the rough falls in it instead, now you have trouble. The gamble is whether or not to play safely in the fairway, or take chances by hitting near the rough. Sometimes you get away with taking those chances and sometimes you pay the price.

The fairway or the rough—from where would you rather hit a ball? The fair way or the rough way, which would you rather live? What I really mean is, God's way or the world's way? Which would you rather live? Just as it can be tempting in golf to occasionally hit near or over the rough, in life, there are many worldly temptations that look very inviting. In golf, you may get away with hitting from the rough for a while, but you'll never score consistently well if you don't stay in the fairway. In the world, living in sin may be fun for a while, but it will eventually catch up to you.

Hebrews 11: 25 says:

*Choosing rather to suffer affliction with the people of God, then to enjoy the pleasures of sin for a season.*

This scripture is in reference to the choice Moses made to live with the Hebrews rather than enjoy the pleasures of the Pharaoh's palace. What this scripture says to us is the pleasures of sin are only for a short time. They don't last. Just in case you have mistakenly read into this scripture that your choices are to have pleasure in sin or stay clear of sin and suffer affliction, then you need to read this next scripture.

Psalm 16:11 says:

*Thou wilt shew me the path of life: in thy presence is fulness of joy; at thy right hand are pleasures for evermore.*

> Thou wilt show me the path of life: in thy presence is fullness of joy; at thy right hand are pleasures for evermore.
> Psalm 16:11

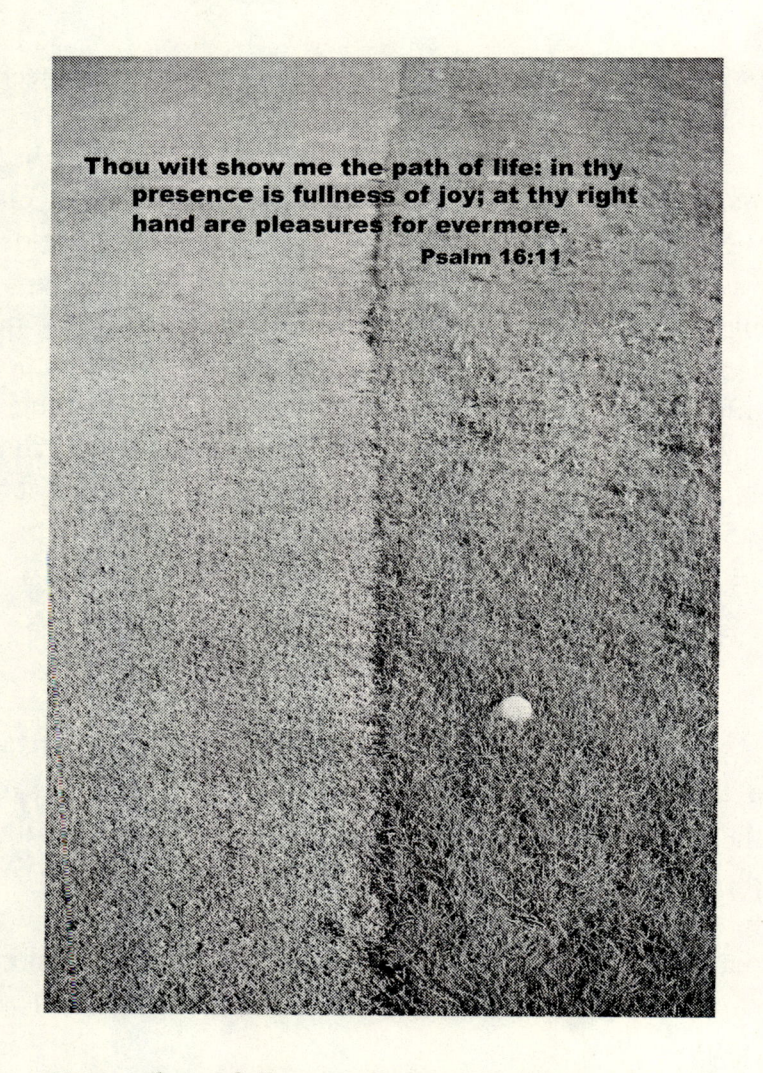

Wow, when I follow God's way he will show me how to live. With Him I will be full of joy, and better yet, his pleasures last forever. As many people who know me well will attest to, I'm not the most intelligent man in the world, but I am certainly smart enough to be able to see an obvious choice when it's placed before me. I can either live in a worldly manner, indulging in sin, and enjoying pleasures for a short time or live in a way that will be pleasing to God, be full of joy, and enjoy pleasures forever. There's a popular expression often used that adequately sums up this choice—"no-brainer." I can't choose for you, but I know I'm going to try to keep the ball in the fairway. When I've finished playing the game, I want my card to reflect the best score I'm capable of shooting.

## Avoid the Hazards

Isaiah 54:17
*No weapon that is formed against thee shall prosper; and every tongue that shall rise against thee in judgment thou shalt condemn. This is the heritage of the servants of the Lord, and their righteousness is of me, saith the Lord.*

I'm ready for my second shot. I look toward the green to decide what club would be best to use in this situation. Holy mackerel! Who designed this golf course? My first shot was right down the middle of the fairway. Isn't my second shot supposed to be easier since I hit my first one so well? On the left I see a ball-swallowing pond. Both to the right and in front of the green I see huge nightmare bunkers. (As a boy growing up we called them sand traps, now they are called bunkers.) To add to all this mess in front of me, there is a small stream running across the fairway that feeds into that ball-swallowing pond. No matter how well I hit the first shot, I still have to face these hazards.

Well, I have to decide how I'm going to play this so I end up on the green and hopefully get my par. Par is the number of shots that the person who designed the golf course thinks it should take you to hit the ball from the tee into the hole on the green. If you play the hole well and hit the ball one less time than the hole was designed for, that is called a birdie. If you play the hole really well and hit the ball two less times than the hole was designed for, that is called an eagle.

## Playing the Game

Three less than par is called a double eagle, but that's almost impossible. To get a double eagle, a golfer has to hit a hole in one on a hole that was designed to be a par four. Double eagles have been accomplished but they are extremely rare. The other end of the scale is where I am more accustomed to scoring. If you play the hole poorly, and hit the ball one more time than it was designed for, that is called a boogie. Two shots more than par is called a double boogie and three shots more is a triple boogie. There is a quadruple boogie but we won't even "go there" as the saying goes.

Do you notice how I've avoided facing these hazards in front of me? Well, the hazards aren't going away so I better decide how to face them. As far as the ball-swallowing pond goes, I know exactly what I'm going to do. My ball seems to have a magnet for water so I will intentionally hit right and avoid it. If I hit too far right and end up in a bunker, at least I have another shot and haven't lost a ball. I would love to avoid both those bunkers, however. I could hit a lay up shot that lands beyond the stream, but in front of the green and the bunkers. This would leave me a short pitch shot onto the green that I can control much better and possibly land close to the hole. Another possibility might be for me to hit this shot long and right toward the back of the green. This way I'm on the green, but I still avoid the bunkers, the stream, and the ball-swallowing pond. That sounds like a plan to me. I'm going for the back right-hand side of the green.

It doesn't take much of an imagination to compare the hazards on the golf course to the hazards of the real world. Hazards, temptations, and sin face each of us every day.

> **For all have sinned and fall short of the glory of God.**
> **Romans 3:23**

Some temptations are more of a hazard for some people than for others. It doesn't matter what the hazard is, whether sex, drugs, alcohol, dishonesty, unfaithfulness, laziness, self-righteousness, or any number of other possibilities. They don't just go away. We can avoid facing our hazards, temptations, and sins as long as we want, but sooner or later we have to face them. Just as I had to decide how to face the hazards on the golf course, we all must decide how we are going to face the hazards of life. Notice that I said "we." Everyone has hazards to face, you, me, and everyone.

Romans 3:23 (NKJV) says:

*For all have sinned and fall short of the glory of God.*

Knowing that the world is full of hazards, temptations, and sins, the task is to develop a plan to try to avoid them. We especially want to develop plans for those hazards that have proven to be weaknesses in our lives. Perhaps I can apply some of the same strategies I used on the golf course to avoid the hazards I face in the world.

Remember that ball-swallowing pond and what I did to avoid it? I know that hitting around water is a problem for me on the golf course. To avoid using my ball retriever and wasting time trying to snatch my ball out of the water, I just hit my ball well away from any ponds, streams, lakes, oceans, or other forms of $H_2O$. This same advice should be applied to any worldly hazard that habitually causes problems. It's a fairly simple principle to understand, but not always as easy to institute.

If alcohol is a hazard, avoid it. If drugs are a hazard, avoid them. If unfaithfulness is a hazard, avoid being in situations that might cause sexual temptations. Avoid whatever the hazard is that leads to a problem. I know outside assistance is sometimes needed to help us overcome worldly hazards and if it's needed, then get it. Along with seeking proper help for facing the world's hazards, don't ever forget two avenues available that have already been mentioned earlier. First, don't leave God out of the solution.

Psalm 55:22 says:

Cast thy burden upon the Lord, and he shall sustain thee: he shall never suffer the righteous to be moved.

Ezekiel 36:25–26 says:

*Then will I sprinkle clean water upon you, and ye shall be clean: from all your filthiness, and from all your idols, will I cleanse you. A new heart also will I give you, and a new spirit will I put within you: and I will take away the stony heart out of your flesh, and I will give you an heart of flesh.*

Second, remember the benefit of having a mentor. A mentor is someone in whom you can confide and feel comfortable enough with that he or she can hold you accountable for your actions. A mentor is someone to call when the temptations of those worldly hazards become too much to handle alone. As I've already demonstrated, I do whatever I can to avoid hazards on the golf course, especially water. I also seek counsel from the people with whom I'm playing to help me face hazards in the best possible way. Both of these strategies work well with worldly hazards.

Another strategy I mentioned when I was trying to decide how to play my second shot to the green was the lay up. The lay up is really a variation of avoidance. I heard a pastor at a conference use the analogy of a football field when explaining this same principle. Just as I suggested, one way to avoid the hazards on the golf course was to lay up or hit my next shot short of the problems, this pastor suggested that if a particular worldly temptation continually creates problems, then stay ten yards away from it. If

# Playing the Game

**Cast thy burden upon the Lord, and He shall sustain thee, . . .**
**Psalm 55:22**

you don't allow yourself to come close to the hazard, it would only make sense that the hazard won't be so much of a problem. Whether you're a golf or football enthusiast, leave a ten-yard cushion or lay up short of problem hazards. Both you and God will be much happier for it.

## Unavoidable Hazards

Psalm 23:4–5
*Yea, though I walk through the valley of the shadow of death, I will fear no evil: for thou art with me; thy rod and thy staff they comfort me. Thou preparest a table before me in the presence of mine enemies: thou anointest my head with oil; my cup runneth over.*

I was fortunate when hitting my second shot to the green. I had some options to avoid the hazards the golf course architect had laid out before me. Unfortunately we have all seen, or even played, some holes on the golf course where there is no avoiding the hazard. When watching professional golfers on television occasionally you'll see a green that is completely surrounded by water except for a small walkway that attaches it to land. I've played a couple of courses with holes like that.

Recently I saw a picture of a golf course in Idaho that is famous for having a floating green. The only way out to it is by a small boat. I really need to see that hole in person some day. I'm sure those masochists who design golf courses must sit in front of their plans thinking,

"All right, I've allowed the golfers a way out on this hole, this hole, and this hole, but on this hole there will be no way out."

On those holes where there is no way out and the hazard is built in as part of the hole, what is a golfer to do? Switching to another sport might be one option, but that's not the answer. Let's look at some ways to attack this problem.

## Playing the Game

First, the holes that present unavoidable hazards look scarier than they really are. Whether it's a tee shot over a pond to get to the fairway or a short par three to an island green, these are shots we've all hit many, many times on the practice tee. Sure the pond wasn't there or the pin we were aiming for wasn't surrounded by water, but the distance was exactly the same. If I can hit my driver, the Big Kahuna, approximately two hundred fifty yards (sometimes a little further if I have the wind with me) why should I worry about hitting over a pond that only stretches one hundred fifty yards? If I can use an eight or nine iron, or even a pitching wedge to hit the green on a par three that has no water, why should the water make the hole any different? The obvious answer to both these hypothetical questions is that it theoretically shouldn't make any difference. I just have to feel confident that I am capable of hitting the shot required to avoid the hazard that the architect thought would gobble up my ball. To be honest, they have gobbled up several of my golf balls, but I still have faith that I'm capable of hitting the shot needed.

Second, it's imperative to keep your focus on the target. If you're trying to hit over a pond to get to the fairway, then your focus should be on the landing area in the fairway. If you're trying to hit the ball onto the green of a par three, whether surrounded by water or not, keep your focus on the green. As soon as your focus in these two circumstances is distracted by water, the sand, the trees, or whatever the hazard is, you have drastically depleted your chance of hitting the shot properly. Your focus must always be on where you would like the ball to land.

Just as on the golf course there are some holes with unavoidable hazards built into them, in the world we occasionally are confronted with situations that present unavoidable hazards. Perhaps there is a fellow worker, who flirts or is promiscuous, or you are in a work situation where co-

**The lord knoweth how to deliver the godly out of temptation . . .**
2 Peter 2:9

workers continually use foul language and tell off-color jokes, or you attend a party where alcohol or drugs are present. Whatever the situation, the hazard, or the temptation, we know that sometimes there is just no avoiding it. Once again there is a strong correlation between how hazards are handled on the golf course and how they can be handled in the world.

First, have confidence that God will help you through any hazards you confront. Just as you must have confidence to hit over unavoidable hazards on the golf course, you must have faith that God won't leave you defenseless as you face unavoidable hazards of the world.

2 Peter 2:9 says:

*The Lord knoweth how to deliver the godly out of temptations, and to reserve the unjust unto the day of judgment to be punished.*

Philippians 4:13 says:

*I can do all things through Christ which strengtheneth me.*

Hebrews 10:35–36 (NIV) says:

*So do not throw away your confidence; it will be richly rewarded. You need to persevere so that when you have done the will of God, you will receive what he has promised.*

And finally, 1 John 4:4 says:

*Ye are of God, little children, and have overcome them: because greater is he that is in you, than he that is in the world.*

Second, just as I had to keep my focus on the green and not the hazard, when we are faced with unavoidable hazards in the world, our focus has to stay on God and not on the hazard.

Psalm 37:39 says:

*But the salvation of the righteous is of the Lord: he is their strength in the time of trouble.*

Psalm 56:11 says:

*In God have I put my trust: I will not be afraid what man can do unto me.*

And finally, Psalm 73:24–25 says:

*Thou shalt guide me with thy counsel, and afterward receive me to glory. Whom have I in heaven but thee? and there is none upon earth that I desire beside thee.*

If we keep our eyes on the Lord and always aim at pleasing him, the temptations of the world won't look quite so tempting.

A third strategy, which was mentioned earlier when I was explaining about the tee box and the use of a tee, is to always use the power of prayer before a hazard is even confronted. If we allow the Holy Spirit to go before us, many of those unavoidable hazards somehow are avoided.

Ephesians 6:10–11&16 says:

*Finally, my brethren, be strong in the Lord, and in the power of his might. Put on the whole armour of God, that ye may be able to stand against the wiles of the devil. Above all, taking the shield of faith, wherewith ye shall be able to quench all the fiery darts of the wicked.*

One last thing I have to mention before walking to the green where I have successfully hit my second shot (remember the fantasy thing). All of the recommendations for facing the hazards of the world have one thing in common. They all include in one form or another, the understanding that the Holy Spirit lives within you. Whether the scripture says the godly, ye are of God, the righteous or child of God, it is assumed that all of the above are true. Consider the options if they aren't a reality in a person's life. I can't even imagine facing the hazards of the world, whether avoidable or unavoidable, without the Holy Spirit on my side.

Let me tell you a truth that somehow is ignored by many either through ignorance or foolishness. If we read the scriptures in the book of Revelation in the Bible, although the devil is strong and wily, Jesus is the winner. As the song goes, there's victory in Jesus, but that victory didn't come cheap.

So which do you want for your life? Do you want to face the hazards of the world knowing that you're on the winning team? I know what I've decided. It may have taken me a while to understand, but I can't even imagine starting the day without the power of God going before me.

# Chapter 4

# On the Green

### SURVEY THE PUTT

Philippians 3:13–14
*Brethren, I count not myself to have apprehended: but this one thing I do, forgetting those things which are behind and reaching forth unto those things which are before. I press toward the mark for the prize of the high calling of God is Christ Jesus.*

Drive for show and putt for dough. That's an old saying used on the professional golfers' tour. I may not be putting for money but the principle behind that old saying still applies. I've made it here onto the green in two shots. Now I have to putt the ball into the hole and finish it off. Have you ever seen the golfers on television as they look over a putt?

First, they stand behind the ball and try to figure which way the ball is going to go. Then they go stand on the opposite side of the green to see if it looks any different from over there. Next they stand to the side of the projected line where their putt is going. Sometimes they will go to the other side again to check things out. Finally they'll get behind the ball one more time, hold their putter up like a plum line (that's a string carpenters use to make sure things are straight).

Then and only then, after examining every blade of grass between their ball and the cup, they stand in position to putt the ball in the hole. If we amateurs took all that time for each putt, the group playing behind us would be hollering in no time flat. So considering that I am very much an amateur, I squat down once behind my ball, try to see if there is any slope to the green, and stand up to the ball ready to putt.

What are golfers really looking for as they examine the greens before they putt? This careful ritual of examining the green is supposed to expose hidden secrets within the grass. Is the ball going to turn to the right or is it going to turn to the left? Perhaps it is going to do both and really surprise the unknowing golfer. Is the putt uphill or downhill? Will the ball speed up as it rolls toward the hole, or will it slow down? Will the grain of the grass tend to make the ball move one way or another? All of the above are considerations that go through a golfer's mind as he or she decides exactly how to hit the putt on its way to the hole. But me, I squat down once behind my ball, try to see if there is any slope to the green and stand up to the ball ready to putt.

When I think about the way some golfers examine the path of their golf ball across a finely manicured green, I become saddened somewhat, to think that the majority of those same golfers probably don't take nearly as much time to examine the paths of their own lives. Imagine all of the poor decisions that could be avoided if people used the same type of meticulous care in examining their options in everyday circumstances. A quick look at my own past convicts me of the same sort of hazardous decision-making in my own life. Fortunately there is a way to examine the paths our lives will take that assures us of never having to live with regrets. Why didn't someone tell us this before? Well, probably someone was trying to tell us. The problem is, each of us must be receptive to hearing the message.

First, as hard as it is to do, give God the decision-making power. Our worldly upbringing often runs contrary to this principle. One only has to look at how we can mess up the decision-making process to convince us that it's way past time to try something different.

Proverbs 3:5–6 says:

*Trust in the Lord with all thine heart; and lean not unto thine own understanding. In all thy ways acknowledge him, and he shall direct thy paths.*

Human nature makes us want to try to work out all our problems ourselves. Often we look at life-changing decisions with a self-serving, self-pleasing attitude. When we realize the decision was wrong all we can say is, "Why me?" Trusting God to lead us in the paths we should travel surely would eliminate an awful lot of heartache, not to mention save families, money, homes, jobs, and lives in general.

Isaiah 42:16 says:

*And I will bring the blind by a way that they knew not; I will lead them in paths that they have not known; I will make darkness light before them, and crooked things straight. These things will I do unto them, and not forsake them.*

Hopefully by now the question has come to your mind, "All right, I'll let God be my decision maker but how do I do that?"

I'm glad you asked. We've actually talked about the answer several times already. Take all your problems to God in prayer.

Philippians 4:6 says:

*Be careful for nothing; but in everything by prayer and supplication with thanksgiving let your requests be made known unto God.*

What a huge step of faith to go from someone who tries to control his or her own life to someone who places his or her life before the Lord and allows him to take control. Sure it is a huge step of faith, and a little scary for someone who has never trusted in the Lord. But think of the benefits in trying.

Isaiah 26:12 (NIV) says:

*Lord, you establish peace for us; all that we have accomplished you have done for us.*

Psalm 29:11 says:

*The Lord will give strength unto his people; the Lord will bless his people with peace.*

And finally, John 14:27 says:

*Peace, I leave with you, my peace I give unto you: not as the world giveth, give I unto you. Let not your heart be troubled, neither let it be afraid.*

Wow! I can have peace about my life by going to God in prayer and allowing him to be my decision maker. As simple as that sounds, it's true. There are times when you go to the Lord in prayer and it seems like you wait and wait and wait for an answer. That may happen, but if it does then you have to decide whether or not what you're considering is really in God's will. God isn't going to send you an e-mail message or a plane with a banner to supply your answers for you. What God will do, however, according to Philippians 4:7 is:

*And the peace of God, which passeth all understanding, shall keep your hearts and minds through Christ Jesus.*

That's right, God will give you a peace that you can feel within, and you will know that you are in God's will. When an uneasy feeling accompanies the decision-making process, one has to question whether or not God is a part of that decision. If we ask ourselves before making any decision, "How will God feel about this?" then we will usually be one step closer to making the right decisions in our life.

There it is, the answer to how to manage our lives without regrets. Pray to God, let him be the decision maker, and always ask, "Is this what God would want for me?" God will let you know his will in your life, not with lightning bolts or supernatural miracles (although he could if he wanted), but with peace that only God can provide.

All right, I've looked over this putt long enough. It's time to see what I can do with it. I have an idea before I hit it though. Earlier I quoted Proverbs 3:5&6. The New Inter-

> Trust in the Lord with all thine heart; and lean not unto thine own understanding. In all thy ways acknowledge Him, and He shall direct thy paths.
>
> Proverbs 3:5,6

national Version of this same scripture might help me right now. It ends saying, "In all ways acknowledge him, and he will make your paths straight." I wonder if God can straighten out this putt for me?

## Lag It Up There

Psalm 145: 18
*The Lord is nigh unto all them that call upon him, to all that call upon Him in truth.*

I'm approximately twenty-five feet from the cup. I've looked over the green carefully. It looks like a fairly straight putt with maybe a little turn to the right just as the ball approaches the hole. I realize, if I were a professional, I'd be thinking about making this putt. Believe me, I'm no professional. My mind is telling me, "It would be nice to make this, but if I keep it close to the hole, I can put the next one in and get a par." What I want to do is hit a lag putt that will roll up there nice and close to the cup.

Several years ago I heard Arnold Palmer discussing his putting technique. Many golfers use the same theory as Arnie, and it just stuck with me when he said it. On a long putt he mentally draws a three-foot radius circle around the hole. When he putts, his goal is to end up somewhere in that circle, thus leaving a fairly short second putt for par. This putt, where you want to keep it close to the hole, is called a lag putt. When golf course architects design each hole, they figure two putts on each green. One putt gets the ball close and one puts it in the hole.

Amateurs, like myself, strive to two putt every green on the course. Professionals average well below two putts per hole. No one, whether amateur or professional likes to see three putt greens. So here I am, my goal is to lag it up there, keep it close to the hole and assure myself of walking away with a par.

I look at a lag putt as the way I want to live my whole life. I know I'm not perfect. I know I'm going to falter and fall short of my goal to be sinless before God. However, if I live like a lag putt and try to stay as close to the Lord as I can, I know the Lord will honor me for my efforts.

James 4:8 says:

*Draw nigh to God, and he will draw nigh to you.*

How's that for assurance? If I try to stay close to God, he will stay close to me. Knowing how Satan has hazards every place we turn, or traps, it certainly is reassuring to know that God is close to me. A few years ago there was a movie called *My Body Guard*. That's how I think of God. My bodyguard, God, is the creator of all things. How can it get any better than that?

Psalm 119:169 says:

*Let my cry come near before thee: deliver me according to thy word.*

Another wonderful benefit of staying close to God is that it enables me to be more receptive to his will in my life. Earlier I discussed the need to allow God to be the decision maker in our lives. If we don't stay close to God, we won't always be aware of what he's trying to say to us.

Deuteronomy 6:27 says:

*Go thou near, and hear all that the Lord our God shall say: and speak thou unto us all that the Lord our God shall speak unto thee; and we will hear it, and do it.*

## On the Green

Finally, staying close to God allows me to be a better witness for him. Let's face it, the world is always looking at Christians with a microscopic eye. Although we know we're not perfect, the world expects us to be. Typically heard criticism includes things like, "He says he's a Christian, but I see what he's really like," or "Why should I go to church, I know how some of those hypocrites live?" I think we've all heard the saying, "Christians aren't perfect, they're just saved." We certainly can't use that as an excuse for not striving toward being closer and closer to the Lord. Remember that the world expects perfection. No, we may not be perfect, but the world should see a difference in us. It should be the goal of each person who professes to be a Christian that his or her life would reflect the love of God through them.

> **Go thou near, and hear all that the Lord our God shall say . . .**
> **Deuteronomy 6:27**

John 1:7 says:

*He came as a witness to testify concerning the light, so that through him all men might believe.*

Jesus says in Acts 1:8:

*But ye shall receive power, after that the Holy Ghost is come upon you: and ye shall be witnesses unto me both in Jerusalem, and in all Judaea, and in Sama'ria, and unto the utter most part of the earth.*

And finally, Isaiah 43:12 says:

*. . . Ye are my witnesses, saith the Lord, that I am God.*

Sure, we may not be perfect and we know that we will fall short of the glory of God, but we have a responsibility to strive to be the best that we can. We have a responsibility to be the best witness for the Lord that we can. One way to be the best witness possible is to stay close to God. Live your life like a lag putt. Stay as close as you can.

## It's a Gimmie—Or Is It?

Romans 5:15 (NIV)
*But the gift is not like the trespass. For if the many died by the trespass of the one man, how much more did God's grace and the gift that came by the grace of the one man, Jesus Christ, overflow to the many!*

Yes, my lag putt ended up exactly where I wanted. I have a short six-inch putt to get a par on the first hole. That's how I like to start a round of golf. Of course the birdie would have been nice, but I'm a happy man right now. My playing partners just told me my last putt was a gimmie. That was nice of them. A gimmie is a short putt, close enough to the hole that your playing partner or partners concede it to you. In other words, they figure you're going to make it so they give it to you without the putt actually having to be tapped in the hole.

When playing with friends or in a match play tournament, gimmies are allowed. Match play refers to two players competing against each other for the hole. They can concede a putt to their competitor and call it a gimmie. In stroke play tournaments, each individual stroke counts, so there are no gimmies. I appreciate the confidence my friends have in me to sink a six-inch putt. I will graciously accept the gimmie and walk off the first green with a par.

Our eternal destiny is very similar to a tournament using stroke play. There are no gimmies in regard to eternal life in heaven. It doesn't matter how close we come to perfection in our lives, there are no gimmies into the kingdom of God.

Matthew 7:13–14 (NIV) says:

*Enter through the narrow gate. For wide is the gate and broad is the road that leads to destruction, and many enter through it. But small is the gate and narrow the road that leads to life, only a few find it.*

The road that leads to life is the road to heaven, and only a few find it because there are no gimmies. There are those who think if they go to church every Sunday and serve on all the right committees their salvation must be guaranteed. Don't get me wrong, going to church and serving the needs of committees is important, but it certainly doesn't have anything to do with acceptance into heaven.

James 1:26–27 (NIV) says:

*If anyone considers himself religious and yet does not keep a tight rein on his tongue, he deceives himself and his religion is worthless. Religion that God our Father accepts as pure and faultless is this: to look after orphans and widows in their distress and to keep oneself from being polluted by the world.*

Jesus, himself, says in Matthew 7:21 (NKJV):

*Not everyone who says to Me, "Lord, Lord," shall enter the kingdom of heaven.*

Whoa, there's something to really think about! Not everyone who says, "Lord, Lord," shall enter into heaven and you have to keep yourself from being polluted by the world. Certainly giving to charities, never hurting but helping others, and volunteering your time whenever asked must help one get into heaven.

Ephesians 2:8–9 says:

*For by grace ye are saved by faith; and that not of yourselves: it is the gift of God: Not of works, least any man should boast.*

Titus 3:5–6 says:

*Not by works of righteousness, which we have done, but according to his mercy he saved us, by the washing of regeneration, and renewal of the Holy Ghost Which he shed on us abundantly through Jesus Christ our Savior.*

And 2 Timothy 1:9 says:

*Who hath saved us, and called us with an holy calling, not according to our works, but according to his own purpose and grace, which was given us in Christ Jesus before the world began.*

Does this mean we can do whatever we want because it has no effect on whether we go to heaven or not? Of course that's not what it means.

Titus 3:8 says:

*This is a faithful saying, and these things I will that thou affirm constantly, that they which have believed in God might be careful to maintain good works. These things are good and profitable to men.*

And James 2:26 says:

*For as the body without the spirit is dead, so faith without works is dead.*

Do we all get the picture now? We're expected to do good works if we want to please God. God will bless us for our good works, but it's not those works that assure us eternal life in heaven.

Finally, I know there are some who believe that since God is a loving father, he forgives us for our sins and we all enter heaven because of his forgiveness. I'm sorry to say it isn't quite that easy. God does love us. He loves us with a love far greater than I can understand. God loves us so much that he gave his only son to die for us. God will forgive us for our sins too, but forgiveness is not automatic. Forgiveness isn't automatic because besides loving us, God is also just.

Romans 2:5–9 says: (NIV)

*But because of your stubbornness and your unrepentant heart, you are storing up wrath against yourself for the day of God's wrath, when his righteous judgment will be revealed. God will give to each person according to what he has done. To those who by persistence in doing good seek glory, honor and immorality, he will give eternal life. But for those who are self-seeking and who reject the truth and follow evil, there will be wrath and anger. There will be trouble and distress for every human being who does evil.*

Hmmm, God loves us, he will forgive us for our sins, but his forgiveness is not automatic. Well then, how do we have eternal life in heaven? I was waiting for you to ask that question.

Listen to the answer in this next piece of scripture. Romans 6:23 says:

*For the wages of sin is death; but the gift of God is eternal life through Jesus Christ our Lord.*

The gift of God is eternal life through Jesus. "Through Jesus," must be the key because we've heard that a few times now. Even in Romans 2:8, which we read just a minute ago, it said, "those who are self seeking and those who reject the truth."

In John 14:6, Jesus says:

*I am the way, the truth, and the life: no man cometh unto the Father, but by me.*

Jesus is the truth; he's the way, our way to God and eternal life in heaven.

Ephesians 1:7 (NKJV) says:

*In Him (meaning Jesus) we have redemption through His blood, the forgiveness of sins.*

There's the forgiveness of sins. It comes through the blood of Jesus. Why does forgiveness come through Jesus? Why is Jesus the key to eternal life in heaven?

Let's take a quick look at the Bible. Remember, I'm not a Bible scholar, but this is how I understand things from what I've read and learned. God made a perfect world in the Garden of Eden. Adam and Eve violated the trust God had in them by allowing themselves to be deceived by Satan and they committed sin. God banished Adam and Eve from the garden and said they and all generations after them would have to produce their own food from the land. Adam and Eve had many children, and their children had many children. We know Adam taught his children about God because they worshiped him and made sacrifices to him.

Unfortunately, just as in the world today, some of the people believed in God and many did not. The world became extremely corrupt, except for one man we've all heard of, Noah. God was disgusted with the actions of the people, all but Noah. God spoke to Noah and told him to build an ark in preparation for a great flood that would destroy all life on the earth. Noah obeyed God, built the ark, and filled it with two of every kind of animal along with his family. When the flood came, all life on the earth was destroyed, except for Noah, his family, and the animals on the ark. When the flood subsided and Noah opened the doors of the ark so that they could replenish life on earth. God made a covenant with Noah. As a sign to the world that he would never destroy the earth by flooding it again, God said he would put a rainbow in the sky.

God also said he would demand an accounting from each man and woman. Throughout the entire Old Testament, God reveals to us his plan to send a Messiah to save the world. Save the world from what? Save the people of the world from an eternal life separated from God. There are almost fifty references to the Messiah in the Old Testament. Not that they aren't all interesting, but here is a list of some of the most interesting of these.

Psalm 2:7–8 says the Messiah will be the Son of God.
Micah 5:2 says the Messiah will be born in Bethlehem.
Isaiah 7:14 says the Messiah will be born of a virgin.
Isaiah 53:1–12 describes the life and death of the Messiah.
Psalm 22:16 discusses the pierced hands and feet and Psalm 22:18 discusses the casting of lots for the garments of the Messiah.

All of these references to the Messiah, found in the Old Testament, were written hundreds of years before the birth of Jesus to a virgin named Mary, in a town called Bethlehem. It was Jesus who declared himself to be the Son of God and was betrayed by those who loved him. And it was Jesus whose hands and feet were pierced as the Roman soldiers cast lots for his clothes. The other references to the Messiah found in the Old Testament will only further testify to the fact that Jesus is indeed the one who God was revealing to the world.

So what was Christ's purpose on earth? How was Jesus going to save the world from a life without God? The Old Testament also gives us clue after clue about Christ's purpose here on earth. One of the most well known scriptures that foretells Christ's purpose is in Genesis 22, in which God asks Abraham to sacrifice his son Isaac as a burnt offering. It is emphasized in the Bible that this was Abraham's one and only son. When Abraham obeyed God and was about to sacrifice Isaac, God provided a ram as a substitute.

Another well-known scripture that also foretells Christ's purpose on earth is Exodus 12. Leading up to Exodus 12, Moses is arguing with the Pharaoh of Egypt to let the Hebrews go from slavery. The Pharaoh keeps resisting, so God finally tells Moses he is going to send a plague over all Egypt that will kill the first born son of every family. Notice again the reference to the firstborn son. The Hebrews were instructed to put the blood of a lamb on the doorframes of their homes so the plague would pass over them. Based on this, Passover was instituted.

A quick review at this point might put everything into perspective. God loves us but he can't allow sin into heaven. All of us are sinners and don't deserve to live in such a perfect place as heaven. Remember we read that the price for sin is death. This is not a literal death, but life without God, which is worse than any form of death that we can imagine.

Again, God loves us so much, he doesn't want to see us die or be separated from him. In the greatest act of love ever known, God has provided someone else to die in our place and that someone was Jesus. Jesus died so we won't have to. The main purpose for Jesus to come to earth was to be that sacrificial, substitutionary lamb. God only asks one thing of us so that we might be saved from eternal separation or death. God asks that we love his son, that we love Jesus. He asks that we receive Him as our Savior (the one who saves us from death).

Romans 10:9 says: (NKJV)

*If you confess with your mouth the Lord Jesus and believe in your heart that God has raised Him from the dead, you will be saved.*

## On the Green

There are no gimmies into heaven. It doesn't matter how religious a person is or how many wonderful things he or she has done. Put your name into John 3:16 and receive God's forgiveness today and forever.

For God so loved (your name) that He gave His only begotten Son that (your name) believing in Him should not perish but have everlasting life.

> Not everyone who says to me, "Lord, Lord," shall enter the kingdom of heaven.
> Matthew 7:21

## Chapter 5

# Odds and Ends

### TOO BIG FOR MY BRITCHES
### (AND NOT FROM EATING)

1 Peter 4:16
*Yet if any man suffer as a Christian, let him not be ashamed; but let him glorify God on this behalf.*

As I come to the second tee, I'm all pumped up. I started with a par. I feel like a pro. I'm ready for the tour (For you non-golfers, that's the Professional Golfers' Tour.) I'm on top of the world. I'm up first on the second hole because I'm the man; I'm the par man. I take the ball and the tee out of my pocket and strut my stuff as I walk up to the tee box. Into the ground goes the tee with the ball perched on top of it. I take my stance, look down at the ball and I know this is my day. Slowly I bring the big Kahuna back (remember, that's my one wood, the driver). There is no doubt in my mind this ball is headed close to three hundred yards down the middle of the fairway.

Swing, swoosh, dribble, dribble, dribble. I topped the ball. That means I hit too high and it never left the ground. The ball went straight down the fairway all right, but only about thirty yards. What happened to my day? What happened to my three hundred yard drive? What happened to my being the man?

If you have ever golfed, you know the type of shot I just described. I've even seen professionals top the ball occasionally. There is nothing like the game of golf to teach humility.

Here I was, so sure this was my day to shoot the lowest round of golf ever seen at this course. Naturally I know better. I know what my average score is. But somehow for a moment I just forgot who I really was. There are a couple of Biblical lessons that immediately come to mind in regard to this situation in which I've put myself.

Proverbs 27:1–2 says:

*Boast not thyself of tomorrow; for thou knowest not what a day may bring forth. Let another man praise thee, and not thine own mouth; a stranger and not thine own lips.*

In my case I didn't have to wait a day to see what would come forth. I only had to wait a couple of minutes while I went to the next hole and made a fool of myself. I can't believe I was so silly. But this was only a golf game. What about in our daily lives? How easy it is to become consumed with one's own accomplishments! Satan is cunning and he'll get a person so hung up on him or herself that God suddenly isn't a part of the mind set. I personally believe that God made our shoulder joint the way he did just so we couldn't reach around and pat ourselves on the back. When we start thinking about how wonderful we are because of the great things we've done, we lose sight of the fact that to God goes the glory. Without Him our accomplishments are meaningless and worthless.

Matthew 23:12 says:

*And whosoever shall exalt himself shall be abased; and he that shall humble himself shall be exalted.*

Abased, according to Mr. Webster in his handy *College Dictionary*, means to be reduced in rank or estimation. Needless to say, my estimation of myself was reduced after that golf shot, but again that was only a game. The effects of being humbled by the Lord in the real world can be much more devastating than being a little red faced in front of your friends. The Lord wanted us to understand this point so much that he repeats it almost word for word again in Luke 14:11 and in Luke 18:14. I'm not the smartest man in the world, but I am smart enough to know that if someone tells you something three times, it is probably important. We especially want to listen if the someone speaking happens to be God.

Now that I've established the fact that I unknowingly allowed myself to get too big for my britches, I have to wonder how it happened? I love the Lord and I try to follow his will for my life. So, how did I become so consumed with myself? Well, I think I know the answer. I lost my concentration—not my concentration on golf, but my concentration on God.

Whether at work or recreation, God still needs to be first and foremost in our minds. Everything we do should be assessed by one thing. How would God feel about my doing this? Certainly, if I had kept that in mind as I approached the second tee I would have known God didn't approve of my foolish boastfulness. Satan, in many devious ways, will try to distract us from living the way God wants us to live. One of Satan's ploys is for us to lose our concentration or our mindset on God.

1 Corinthians 7:35 says: (NKJV)

> *And I say this for your own profit, not that I may put a leash on you, put for what is proper, and that you may serve the Lord without distraction.*

The question now is, how do I keep my concentration on the Lord and not on worldly things? How do I keep myself from being distracted by Satan?

**Boast not thyself of tomorrow; for thou knowest not what a day may bring forth. Let another man praise thee, and not thine own mouth; a stranger and not thine own lips.**
**Proverbs 27:1,2**

Psalm 16:8 says:

*I have set the Lord always before me: because he is at my right hand.*

2 Samuel 22:4 (NKJV) says:

*I will call upon the Lord, who is worthy to be praised: so shall I be saved from mine enemies.*

And finally Psalm 34:1 says:

*I will bless the Lord at all times: his praise shall continually be in my mouth.*

God really makes things simple if we only follow his directions. If I always set the Lord before me and keep his praises upon my lips, then who will always be on my mind and be reflected in my actions? Duh, that's a no-brainer.

1 Chronicles 16:15 says:

*Be ye mindful always of his covenant; the word which he commanded to a thousand generations.*

The more we put God first in our lives and keep His praises on our lips, the easier and easier it gets. Finally we get to a point where we don't consciously think about it. It just becomes a part of our lives.

Now that I have my priorities back in order, God first and me second, I have to figure out how I'm going to make up for being such a jerk. Let's see, how am I going to hit this next shot?

## Thank God for Mulligans

Romans 10: 9
*That if you shall confess with your mouth the Lord Jesus and shall believe in your heart that God has raised him from the dead, you shall be saved.*

My playing partners have all hit their tee shots and told me to use a mulligan. Since this is just a friendly game between buddies, I think I'll take them up on their offer. We usually allow each other one mulligan per nine holes. A "mulligan" is the opportunity to take your tee shot over without a penalty. When you're playing with friends, mulligans are allowed. I even encourage people, especially golfers with high handicaps, to use mulligans. The point of playing golf is to have fun, enjoy yourself, and try to improve each time you're out on the course. Usually, taking a mulligan keeps you from getting too frustrated and helps you improve on your poor shots.

Notice how I said *usually*. Taking a mulligan doesn't do a whole lot of good if your second shot is as bad as the first (most golfers have been there before). Mulligans aren't allowed in tournaments, unless it's a local fund-raising tournament. At local tournaments played to raise funds for a charity, the sponsors often sell mulligans. For five or ten dollars apiece, you can buy the opportunity to hit a second shot when the first one wasn't so great. I usually like to save my mulligans for times when I really need them. I hate using a mulligan this early in the round, but since my friends offered, I'm going over.

## Odds and Ends

A mulligan in golf makes me think of the salvation we have in Jesus Christ our Lord. When we put our faith in the Lord Jesus, God gives us a mulligan; he gives us a chance to start over without penalty.

Romans 6:4–10 (NIV) says:

> *We were therefore buried with him through baptism into death in order that, just as Christ was raised from the dead through the glory of the Father, we too may live a new life. If we have been united with him in his death, we will certainly also be united with him in his resurrection. For we know that our old self was crucified with him so that the body of sin might be rendered powerless, that we should no longer be slaves to sin—because anyone who has died has been freed from sin. Now if we died with Christ, we believe that we also live with him. For we know that since Christ was raised from the dead, he can not die again; death no longer has mastery over him. The death he died, he died to sin once for all; but the life he lives, he lives to God.*

Isn't that the most unbelievable news you've ever heard? When we put our faith in Jesus Christ, our old self is crucified with him. Just as he lives, we too live a new life. Our old body of sin is powerless and we are no longer slaves to sin.

2 Corinthians 5:17 says:

> *Therefore if any man be in Christ, he is a new creature: old things are passed away; behold, all things are become new.*

God makes his mulligan available to everyone, high and low handicappers alike—that is people of all levels. It's one offer that should be easy to accept even if we don't deserve it.

Another thought that comes to mind when I think of mulligans is the way God forgives us for our sins. When we accept Christ as our Savior, our sins—past, present, and future—are paid for through his crucifixion. Does that mean we don't have to ask God's forgiveness when we sin? Obviously, the answer is no. Think about it. God has forgiven us for our sins by having his son die in our place and then we thank him by sinning and saying nothing to him about it. If we truly love the Lord, it should ache our heart to know that we've hurt him by sinning. Praying to God and asking his forgiveness is something that should be as natural as breathing. And again, in an act of love greater than any we can imagine, God forgives us and wipes the slate clean.

Isaiah 43:25 says:

*I, even I, am he that blotteth out thy transgressions for mine own sake, and will not remember thy sins.*

Jeremiah 31:34 says:

*I will forgive their iniquity, and I will remember their sins no more.*

And in the New Testament, 1 John 1:9 says:

*If we confess our sins, he is faithful and just to forgive us our sins, and to cleanse us from all unrighteousness.*

Once again, what a wonderful mulligan the Lord has provided for all who would simply ask. When we sin, we ask his forgiveness and he blots it out of his mind. We get to start over without any penalty. I know what some of you are saying to yourselves, "But you don't know me. I've really separated myself from the Lord. There's no way God could forgive me for all I've done to hurt him." By the grace of God you're wrong.

2 Chronicles 30:9 says:

*The Lord your God is gracious and merciful, and will not turn away his face from you, if you return unto him.*

Hosea 14:4 says:

*I will heal their backsliding, I will love them freely: for my anger is turned away from him.*

And Malachi 3:7 says:

*Return unto me, and I will return unto you, says the Lord of hosts.*

God understands us better than we even understand ourselves. He knew us before we were even conceived. It doesn't matter the amount of our sin because God forgives us and loves us. Remember I said earlier that it doesn't pay to use a mulligan if you don't take advantage of it. Well, I'm going to use the mulligan God has provided for me and I intend to make the most of it.

# Golfing with God

. . . just as Christ was raised from the dead through the glory of the Father, we too may live a new life.

                                        **Romans 6:4**

## The Refreshment Cart

Isaiah 1: 18
*Come, let us reason together, says the Lord: though your sins be as scarlet, they shall be white as snow; though they be red as crimson, they shall be as wool.*

Here comes the refreshment cart! I need something to refresh me after the way I started this hole. Not all courses have refreshment carts, but many do. This is one amenity that's not reserved for just the more exclusive courses. The refreshment cart is like a mini canteen truck. They carry drinks of all types, cookies, crackers, sandwiches, and sometimes even fruit. Of course, it goes without saying that since the golfers are a captive audience, the prices are usually outrageous. Outrageous at least compared to the prices you would pay in a regular store. But when you're golfing and you're hungry or hot, somehow the price seems reasonable enough to pay. For some reason the golf courses always hire women to drive the refreshment carts. I'm not sure why unless it's to prey on a man's libido. Often the women are young, but sometimes they're older too. There are women golfers so why don't they hire some men as refreshment cart drivers? Oh well, that's not something I'm concerned with. I'm just going to have bottled water for now—something to quench my thirst and keep my throat from being dry. I said bottled water for now because we'll see the refreshment cart several times today as we play our round of golf. The woman driving the cart drives around and around the course making sure the golfers have whatever they'd like from her little restaurant on wheels. The only time she goes in is to refill her cart with anything she has run out of. So, it's water for now. Maybe I'll buy something else the next time we meet a few holes from now.

When I see the refreshment cart coming I think of the way God would like us to honor him. Praising God is not a once-a-week thing to do only on Sundays, or even a twice-a-week thing if we add in Wednesday church services. The name of Jesus should be in our mind and on our lips continually. We should take a refreshment break several times a day to praise and honor God the Father, God the Son, and God the Holy Spirit.

1 Thessalonians 5:16–18 says:

*Rejoice evermore. Pray without ceasing. In every thing give thanks: for this is the will of God in Christ Jesus concerning you.*

Psalms 71:8 says:

*Let my mouth be filled with thy praise and with thy honour all the day.*

And Psalms 35:28 says:

*And my tongue shall speak of thy righteousness and of thy praise all the day long.*

Before you get all excited and tell me there is no way you could follow those scriptures and accomplish anything else during the day, let me tell you what I think God is saying to us. I think what God means is that we should maintain a Godly state of mind in all we say and do. If our

# Odds and Ends

**Let my mouth be filled with thy praise and with thy honor all thy day.**
                                            **Psalms 71:8**

words are spoken in a Godly manner they will be spoken as in prayer. If our actions are done in a Godly manner then they will be honorable to the Lord. Our words and actions can be executed in such a way that they praise God continually.

I do think that along with maintaining a Godly demeanor, we should try to remember God in all we do—remembering to take the time to thank, honor, and praise him often each day. Let me give you some simple examples of what I mean. Naturally, before every meal we should give thanks for the food we eat. If someone you meet is a blessing to you, take the time to thank God for the opportunity of making his or her acquaintance. When you travel, take time to thank God for watching over you and your loved ones. If you should see someone in need of prayer, take the time to bring him or her before the Lord. And finally, sometimes just say, "Thank you Lord for giving me this day and the opportunity to serve you." These are only a few examples of refreshment breaks that we should all take for the sake of those we meet, for our own spiritual blessings, and most importantly for the glory and honor of our Lord.

Well, I'm going to finish this round of golf, but I'll be taking another refreshment break fairly soon. I hope you will too.

## Have You Used Your GPS Today?

Psalm 73: 23–24
*I am continually with thee; thou hast holden me by my right hand. Thou shalt guide me with thy counsel, and afterward receive me to glory.*

I've mentioned a couple of times the amenities exclusive golf courses and country clubs offer in order to make golfers feel special when playing at their facilities. Although most of my golf is played at public or municipal courses, occasionally I'll join the upper crust and thoroughly enjoy the pampering that goes along with it. Recently, on just such an occasion, my wife and I enjoyed one of the newest technologies being employed by some golf courses. This new toy in the golfing world is the Global Positioning System or G.P.S.

Many of you have heard of road service you can purchase for your motor vehicle that, at the push of a button, can track where your car has broken down. Some of you may even have a security system on your motor vehicle that allows the police to track your vehicle if it is stolen. Well, this is the same technology now being used on golf courses. I know you're thinking, "What do they do, track run away golf carts?" No, it's not for that at all.

Mounted on each golf cart is a computer screen. When you drive up to the first hole the system is activated and you are welcomed to the golf course. As you pull up to the tee box, the computer screen shows you exactly how the hole is laid out from the tee to the green. It shows you the slope of the fairway as well as all the hazards and the distances to each one. After you tee off and drive up to your ball, hopefully in the middle of the fairway, the screen shows the layout of the green and exactly how far it is from your ball to the hole.

Another function in the corner of the screen controls your pace of play. It tells you whether you are playing on pace or behind. Although we didn't have this happen, I assume that if you were too slow the computer screen would probably give you a friendly reminder to speed up a little. No matter where you are on the course, the people in the clubhouse can contact you with a message and you can contact them if the need occurs.

One function that I can't leave out appears after you tee off on the ninth hole. As you drive down the ninth fairway toward your ball, a menu appears on the screen allowing you to order food and drinks in the clubhouse. When you finish the ninth hole and head for the tenth to start the second half of the course, your food will be ready and waiting for you as you pass the club house.

I know there is also a scoring function available on the computer screen used in tournament play. There may even be other functions on the computer that my wife and I were not aware of. Let me tell you, we really felt pampered during that round of golf. I didn't take advantage of the food, and my score will tell you I didn't take advantage of knowing the layouts and distances, but we enjoyed experiencing the newest technology on the golf course.

As we played that round of golf with the Global Positioning System, I couldn't help thinking that it operates in much the same way God does. God knows where we are at all times, including the pace at which we live. We can communicate with God at anytime and he communicates with us. God tries to warn us of the hazards we'll have to confront and provides the weapons we'll need to overcome them. God provides nourishment not only for our bodies but also for our souls. God's been using this technology since the beginning of time and golf courses think it's brand new. From the Old Testament to the New Testament, God assures us of his omnipresence.

Genesis 28:15 (NIV) says:

*I am with you and will watch over you wherever you go, and I will bring you back to this land. I will not leave you until I have done what I promised you.*

Exodus 33:14 says:

*And he said, My presence shall go with you, and I will give you rest.*

Haggai 1:13 (NKJV) says:

*I am with you says the Lord.*

Matthew 28:20 says:

*Teaching them to observe all things I commanded you: and, lo I am with you always, even unto the end of the world.*

And finally, 2 Corinthians 13:11 says:

*Be perfect, be of good comfort, be of one mind, live in peace, and the God of love and peace shall be with you.*

The Global Positioning System and all of the preceding scriptures dramatically underline the real purpose of this entire book. If I can see God in almost every aspect of the game of golf, I certainly should be able to look at my life and do the very same thing. God is with us always. Unfortunately we're not always looking for him. God's comfort and love are always available. Unfortunately we don't always

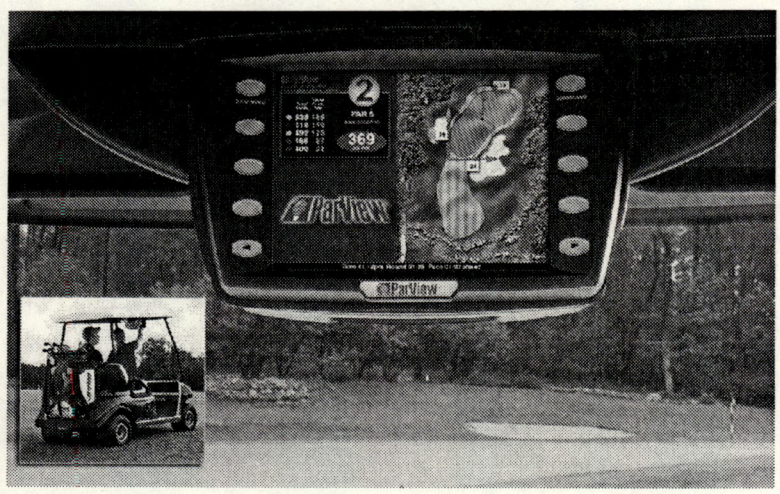

Courtesy of ParView, Inc.

**I am with you and I will watch over you where ever you go . . .**

**Genesis 28:15**

take advantage of such a gift. If you look around at your life and don't see the presence of the Lord, it isn't because he's not there. It's because you've chosen not to recognize him.

Matthew 7:7 says:

*Ask, and it shall be given you; seek and ye shall find; knock, and it shall be opened unto you.*

God really wants to be a part of your life. He loves you and wants you to love him too.
Revelation 3:20 says:

*Behold, I stand at the door, and knock. if any man hear my voice, and open the door, I will come in to him, and will sup with him, and he with me.*

Wouldn't you like to dine with the King of Kings and the Lord of Lords? If you haven't yet opened the door to your life and invited the Lord in, won't you consider doing it today? He's waiting for you to begin an eternal life with him right now.

## SOME FINAL THOUGHTS

John 4: 14
*But whosoever drinks of the water that I shall give him shall never thirst; but the water that I shall give him shall be in him a well of water springing up into everlasting life.*

God has blessed me more than anyone will ever know by giving me the opportunity to share my faith and love for him in this book. Remember however, I'm not a Bible scholar, I'm not a pastor, minister or priest. I'm just a man that loves the Lord. The love I have for the Lord, the unbelievably wonderful life I live with Jesus is available to anyone and everyone who receives Christ as his or her savior. By no means have I pulled out the only worthwhile scriptures from the Bible. Remember all scripture is given by inspiration of God and is profitable to us. If you haven't read your Bible lately, begin today. It's the greatest love story ever told. I pray that the Lord will forgive me for those places where I have drastically simplified his message or words and I hope you will take the time to fill in the gaps with the whole story. I've heard people say, "The Bible is out dated, it's old fashion, it isn't relevant to life today." The Bible is the same yesterday, today, and tomorrow. The message that the Bible has for us is as true today as it was when it was written. Let me close by giving you an example of what I mean.

Joshua brought the Hebrews into the land that God had promised to Moses. He conquered the men of Jericho, the Amorites, the Perizzites, the Canaanites, the Hittites, the

Girgashites, the Hivites, and the Jebusites. And then in his old age, he gathered all the tribes of Israel at Shechem to renew the covenant they had with the Lord. It is now that Joshua spoke the words that so many people have heard and may even have hanging on a wall in there home.

Joshua 24:15 says:

*"And if it seem evil unto you to serve the Lord, choose you this day whom ye will serve; whether the gods which your fathers served that were on the other side of the flood, or the gods of the Amorites, in whose land ye dwell: but as for me and my house, we will serve the Lord."*

Joshua spoke these words thousands of years ago, but the message is just as clear and as potent today. People have to choose who or what they are going to serve. Many people say they believe in God but the question is whether or not they serve Him. Some people serve their job. Some serve money, alcohol, drugs, pornography, illicit sexual affairs, or athletics. Some even serve golf. Most people don't think of themselves as serving these other things but it is where their heart is.

So we must all choose. Just like Joshua said, choose you this day whom you will serve, whether the gods your fathers served or the ones you have made for yourself. But I will tell you this, as for me and my house, we will serve the Lord.

May God bless you all!

## Odds and Ends

2 Tim 1:8 *Do not be ashamed, therfore, about bearing witness to our Lord...*
Let people know who's team you're playing on.
Written by Doug Tatro to share both his love of golf, but more importantly his love for Christ. Great for both non-golfers and golfers alike.

Anvil Cotton deluxe solid 6-panel Brushed Twill cap one size fits all. Available in white and royal.

Cobra Cotton Visor.
Garment washed, cotton twill, velcro closure. One size fits all.

Hanes 50/50 pre shrunk fabric for exceptional value, pearl buttons, welt collar and rib-knit cuffs. Generous specs for a comfortable fit. Available in white, lt. blue, and royal.

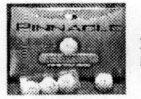

GWG logo golf balls.
Pinnacle Gold Distance, soft, fast core and blended cover to provide golfers with superior distance, straight flight, and durability.

GWG Golf Combo Pack
4 tees, 1 ball marker and a divot tool.

**Visit us at WWW.golfingwithgod.com**

| Qty | Item | Size | Color | Unit Cost | Total |
|---|---|---|---|---|---|
| | Book--Golfing With God | N/A | N/A | $ 12.95 | |
| | Golfing With God Hanes Polo Golf Shirt | Please Circle one Sm Med Lg. XL | Please Circle one White Lt.Blue Royal | $ 24.95 | |
| | Golfing With God Golf Hat | One size fits all | Please Circle one White Royal | $ 16.95 | |
| | Golfing With God Golf Visor | One size fits all | Please Circle one White Royal | $ 15.95 | |
| | Pinnacle Gold Spin GWG Balls 3 pack | N/A | N/A | $ 7.95 | |
| | Pinnacle Gold Spin GWG Balls 15 pack | N/A | N/A | $ 35.95 | |
| | GWG Golf Combo Pack 4 Tees, 1 Marker, 1 Divot Tool | N/A | N/A | $ 2.95 | |
| Mail to: Golfing With God Ministries 5537 N. Socrum Loop Rd. #329 Lakeland, FL 33809-4256 | | | Add 6% Florida sales tax | | |
| | | | Shipping & Handling | $ 3.00 | |
| | | | Please allow 4-6 weeks | Total | |

| Name: |
|---|
| Address: |
| City: State: Zip Code: |

Please Give instructions if you would like your book personalized. How did you hear about Golfing With God?

To order additional copies of

*Golfing* WITH
# GOD

Use the convenient order form supplied.

Or please visit our web site at
www.golfingwithgod.com

Also available at: www.amazon.com

Printed in the United States
40474LVS00003B/21